About the Author

Dr. Natasha Josefowitz was a professor of management for thirty years and is an internationally known business consultant and keynote speaker. A late bloomer, she earned her master's degree at age forty and her PhD at fifty.

For ten years she had her own weekly program on public radio and a monthly segment on television. She has also been a guest on numerous radio and TV shows, including *All Things Considered, The Larry King Show,* and *The Dr. Ruth Show,* to name a few.

Dr. Josefowitz is the best-selling author and award-winning poet of nineteen business and poetry books. Her articles and poems have been published in over one hundred journals and magazines, including the *Harvard Business Review,* the *Wall Street Journal, Psychology Today,* the *London Times,* and most major newspapers in the United States. You can read her bimonthly column in the *La Jolla Today* and *San Diego Jewish World* website.

Natasha has received the Living Legacy Award from the Women's International Center and was named by the *San Diego Business Journal* as one of San Diego's "Top Guns."

The Washington Post says: "Natasha Josefowitz is helping her generation, and those that follow, find their way into a successful, meaningful and fun older age...her optimism about aging is inspiring."

Natasha met Dr. Herman Gadon in 1971 in Switzerland, where they taught and consulted as a team. Later, they returned to the United States as professors at the University of New Hampshire, School of Business and Economics. In 1979 they took a sabbatical leave in San Diego,

California, and stayed on, he at University of California, San Diego and she at San Diego State University.

For over thirty-five years, Herman and Natasha were in synch with each other. Together they wrote, taught, consulted, and traveled around the world, giving lectures on cruise ships. Friends said they were joined at the hip. They retired to the White Sands La Jolla, where they walked on the beach and enjoyed being with each other full-time.

This book is about her learning to travel through life alone

Books by Natasha Josefowitz

Paths to Power: A Woman's Guide from First Job to Top Executive, Addison-Wesley Publishing Company, 1980

Is This Where I Was Going? Warner Books, 1982

You're the Boss: A Guide to Managing Diversity with Understanding and Effectiveness, Warner Books, 1985

Natasha's Words for Families, Warner Books, 1986

Natasha's Words for Friends, Warner Books, 1986

Natasha's Words for Lovers, Warner Books, 1986

Fitting In: How to Get a Good Start in Your New Job, (coauthored with Herman Gadon), Addison-Wesley Publishing Company, 1988

A Hundred Scoops of Ice Cream: Tiny Tales, St. Martin's Press, 1988

Over the Hill and Loving the View: Poems to Celebrate Growing Older, Blue Mountain Press, 1991

Managing Our Frantic Lives: A Humorous and Insightful Look at What Makes Our Lives So Hectic, with 10 Strategies for Coping, Blue Mountain Press, 1994

Women's Secrets: Witty Insights into the Thoughts, Feelings, and Dreams of Women, Blue Mountain Press, 1994

Too Wise to Want to Be Young Again: A Witty View of How to Stop Counting the Years and Start Living Them, Blue Mountain Press, 1995

If I Could Touch the Sky…and Other Poems in Children's Voices, Blue Mountain Press, 1997

If I Eat I Feel Guilty, If I Don't I'm Deprived…and Other Dilemmas of Daily Life, Blue Mountain Press, 2001

Sixteen New Ways for Women to Succeed at Work, Blue Mountain Press, 2004

Retirement: Wise and Witty Advice for Making It the Next Great Adventure, Blue Mountain Press, 2005

Been There, Done That, Doing It Better! A Witty Look at Growing Older by a Formerly Young Person, Blue Mountain Press, 2009

Praise for Living Without the One You Cannot Live Without

"This is great for surviving spouses/partners. It is important for individuals to understand that they are not the only ones—what they are going through is normal."

—Kathleen Pacurar
Former President and CEO of San Diego Hospice and the Institute for Palliative Medicine

"Once again, Natasha has distilled into verse the universal feelings of a woman in a particular time of life, connecting her individual sorrow to that of other women experiencing the same loss and transition. That sharing should give solace to other lonely women living through the absence of couplehood."

—Fredda Isaacson
Warner Books Vice-president, Senior Editor, retired

"Bravo, Natasha, for reminding us that even in our darkest moments the power of the human spirit prevails and reaches toward life."

—Mimi Guarneri, MD FACC
Founder and Medical Director, Scripps Integrative Medicine; author, *The Heart Speaks*

"This little gem of a book will sooth the heart of those who grieve, while for those lucky enough to still be in a relationship with the one they cannot live without, this book can be equally valuable in the reassurance it offers, as well as the powerfully important conversations it can stimulate before the opportunity is gone forever."

—Georgia Robins Sadler, BSN, MBA, Ph.D.
Associate Director for Community Outreach at the Moores UCSD Cancer Center

"She is the poet of the simple insight; each poem disarmingly tells the truths we all know but can feel best when she tells them."

—Erving Polster, Ph.D.
Director of the Gestalt Training Center—San Diego; Clinical Professor,
University of California, San Diego (UCSD)

"The reader always feels at one with Natasha, as much when she is overcome with grief and numbing sadness, as when she is finally returning to herself (and to us!) with palpable energy and optimism. We are all ennobled by this wonderfully touching book."

—Saul Levine, MD
Retired Head of Psychiatry, Rady Children's Hospital

Living Without the One You Cannot Live Without

Hope and Healing after Loss

by
Natasha Josefowitz, Ph.D.

Prestwik Poetry Publishing Co.
7486 La Jolla Blvd
Suite 553
La Jolla, California

ISBN: 1484141326
ISBN 13: 9781484141328
Library of Congress Control Number: 2013907876
CreateSpace Independent Publishing Platform
North Charleston, South Carolina

Dedication

To the memory of my husband, Dr. Herman Gadon—
now part of me forever—and to his children, Nicole,
Margaret, and John, who know what an extraordinary
man we all lost.
—Natasha Josefowitz

Acknowledgements

I want to thank my secretary, Erika Pfeiffer, who not
only typed and edited each poem but also added her
feelings and thoughts.
—Natasha Josefowitz

Table of Contents

Lost in the Periphery

After my husband died
I was no longer
the center of anyone's life
nor is anyone
the center of mine
family and friends
are supportive and comforting
but they are peripheral
as I am peripheral
in their lives
they can continue
without me
as I am supposed
to continue
without him
without the one person
I cannot live without

The Phone Call

The phone call came
in the middle
of a peaceful afternoon
"It's the doctor,"
I told my husband
"Pick up the extension
so we both can hear"
the disembodied voice
on the other end of the phone
said something incomprehensible:
"It's cancer."
we asked how long
"Maybe six months."
we both hung up the phones
and looked at each other
in disbelief
the color drained from his face;
my heart was pounding
"It's okay," I said,
"there is nothing we can't do
as long as we're together"
nine months later
he was gone
and all I was left with
were blank sheets of paper
to say
what I could not
tell him anymore

The Waiting Room

We sit in the waiting room
of the doctor's office
there are twenty-two chairs
and half are filled
with patients
and their relatives
those who must be there
to drive home
the newly handicapped person
who comes out still drugged
from the anesthesia
or with a limb
encased in plaster
the waiting room is drab
like all waiting rooms
with outdated magazines
probably donated awhile back
and not replaced
by the busy staff
who took the most recent ones
    home
then forgot
to bring them back
I'm guessing this—
I don't really know
there's a fake palm tree in a corner
and a "no smoking" sign
my husband's name is called
(it is mispronounced)
and I go with him
to fill out the paperwork
it's about allergies and medications
past medical history
and a question
asked apologetically
"Have you filled out a DNR?"
do not resuscitate form
we had; it's in our records

but we should have it with us
next time, we will
the hospital gown is blue paper
and ties in the back
white socks on his feet
a paper bonnet on his head
extremely unattractive
and he is wheeled out
already with an IV in his arm
I ask the nurse to take
my blood pressure too
it's over the top
she says it's worrisome
but I know better
I'm stressed
an hour later
she takes it again
it's almost normal
back in the waiting room
I wait
I try to read (to no avail)
people waiting
someone eating a sandwich
someone on his cell phone
someone asleep
people waiting
finally, the doctor comes out
the surgery went well
I'll be able to take him home
in half an hour
the instructions are given
do not get the bandages wet
come back in three days
my husband leans on me
I had always done the leaning
this is what growing old is about:
leaning against each other

Hospice

It's a hospital room
like all hospital rooms
with an adjustable bed
a call button for the nurse
an air mattress
to prevent bed sores
I sit in a chair
next to his bed
a chair for guests
except I'm the guest
and the person in the bed
is my husband
hooked to an IV
and to some other tubes
protruding from under the bed
    sheets
his eyes are closed
the room is small
it has the usual:
a TV
a table on wheels
a commode
plastic containers with medical
    items
a box of Kleenex
a box of surgical gloves
a tray with a pink plastic pitcher
Styrofoam cups
apple juice
I prefer cranberry
the paraphernalia is depressing
how long are we to be here?
will they know how to reduce the
    pain—
a pain so excruciating
we came here for some relief
it went from a ten to a two

on the pain scale
the price for that is
    unconsciousness
it's called palliative care
to palliate means to treat symptoms
but not attempt to cure
"Mommy will make it all better
with a kiss on the booboo"
except "mommy" feels helpless
dependent and vulnerable
a social worker is available
and so is a spiritual counselor
I can join a grief workshop
but I just want to be alone
with my husband
alone and afraid of an uncertain
    future
the doctor is young
a fellow on his last rotation
I want the supervisor
and the supervisor's supervisor
to tell me
that my husband will get better
that they'll fix him
somehow
none of this feels right
somehow
it all feels wrong
I don't know where to turn
I want to leave
to go somewhere safe
where we can turn back the clock
to when he was healthy
it would be nice
for me to be unconscious, too
for a little while

The Facade

I walk around with a facade
it's like a cardboard replica of me
which I hold up with my two hands
it's what people see
I smile, make small talk
"No, I'm not really doing better,
but thanks for asking."
I can go anywhere with my facade
give a speech, run a meeting
have a pleasant meal with friends
but hugging is not permitted
to hug, one must go behind
the cardboard cutout
where one encounters
mush, a puddle
a pitiable mess
that breaks down in tears
so no hugs
perhaps I need a suit of armor
to encircle me
all around

Still at Hospice

We're still here because
his back is still hurting
he has prostate cancer
metastasized to his bones
so we're here to get some relief
but the relief comes at a cost
opiates put you to sleep
so he lies there, only half-conscious
and as the hours become days
and the pain is only relieved
by increasing the medications
the days are turning into weeks
we came here, believing he would get better
and come home
but instead
he only came home to die
in a different hospital bed
the one in our continuing care unit
two floors up from our apartment
in our retirement community
he can see the ocean from his window
and hear the waves
hospice people come here, too
adjusting the pumps
the nurses are at his bedside
day and night
at first he has trouble talking
then swallowing
then moving
then breathing
and finally
living

The Funeral

We started at the gravesite
I didn't want the casket
sitting in the chapel
with pallbearers, a hearse
so we started at the gravesite
a young man in a navy uniform
played taps
the coffin was draped in a flag
which was carefully folded
by two navy men
into a tight triangle
they gave it to me
I gave it to his son
standing next to me
was this a movie
or was it real?
I was not sure
one red rose lay on the coffin
when they lowered it down
into the grave dug below
what I really wanted to do
was open the casket
and lie down beside him
close the lid
and just end there
end all the pain
the pain now
and the pain
that will be forever
in the unwelcome future
instead I was given a shovel
and threw earth on the coffin
it made a hollow sound
I felt numb, in a strange fog of pain
I don't remember much of the
    service
a blur of words
about my husband
about his gentle nature
his integrity, his wisdom
his accomplishments
which were impressive

his love for me
for his children
and grandchildren
I could not find the man I loved
in all these words
the man I loved
is not in words of praise
he is somewhere inside of me
but all I can feel is his absence
the family went to the private
    dining room
food, people talking
reminiscing, making plans
to see each other again
my side of the family
blending with his side
my husband would have loved it
people should attend their funerals
before they die
to hear the lovely things
said about them
I wish I could believe
that somehow my husband
is seeing all this
that his spirit is hovering
over the proceedings
perhaps we could all meet again
that would be something
to look forward to
my daughter stayed up with me
past midnight
until I fell asleep, exhausted
she had given me Xanax
to get through the funeral
it had helped
I did not collapse—
not visibly, anyway
the collapse was internal
as if all my organs
collapsed together in a heap
inside of me
and I'm this mush, this puddle

this sad woman, looking brave
faking good countenance
shaking hands
thanking for condolences
even smiling
a Xanax smile
that night
long after midnight
I slept
a Xanax sleep

Dismantling His Office

His son came
to dismantle his office
I had not touched anything
still finding some comfort
among familiar objects
his books were packed up first
six boxes shipped to his son
many left on shelves
to be given away
then came the tools
My husband was a tinker
I kept a few
for some unforeseen
repair emergency
his son took some
the maintenance man
took the rest
the hardest to part with

were the personal items
a photo of us on a ship
expired warranties
manuals on how to use
equipment we no longer owned
some toys meant for grandchildren
now too old to want them
a puzzle, a traveling chess set
a magnifying glass
what to keep?
to give away?
to throw out?
there is a pervasive sadness
about objects once owned
and treasured
by a man I loved
that now need to find
usefulness elsewhere

Where Are You?

Give me a sign
blow out the candle
rustle the curtain
make a sound in the wind
touch my cheek
with a breath of air
give me a sign
so I will know
you are here
somewhere with me
please let me feel you
in the room
in the air
in the energy
pulsating in the universe
my love
where are you?

Maybe

Maybe it's all a mistake
maybe it wasn't real
maybe it was a bad dream
maybe it didn't happen
maybe when
I come home tonight
he'll be there, saying
"Hi, how was it?"
and I'll tell him
all about it
except
he wasn't there
and he didn't ask

The Half-Person

Excruciating pain
whole-body pain
searing, sharp
coming at odd moments
stopping my breath
from the suddenness
the terrible missing
the huge gap
the awful hole
he left me with
reeling from the realization
that I'm only half a person
the other half is gone
the other half is dead
we were one together
a unit, yin and yang
a whole side of me
has been torn away
and it's bleeding
from the open, ragged wound
it's not a clean cut
it's pieces of heart
and pieces of gut
brain cells
that explains why
I'm not functioning as well
why I'm forgetful
at times confused
with a fog in my head
the sharp pain recedes at times
leaving a constant ache
a whole-body ache
both dull and dulling

The Tears Are There Forever

The tears are there
right behind the eyes
ready to spill
at the least provocation
such as a hug
or people saying they're sorry
crying does not help
it relieves nothing
being busy does
concentrating on something
I miss him
rustling the newspapers
in the room next door
his voice on the phone—
I always knew which of the children
he was talking to—
the sound of the shower running
or of his footsteps
in the hallway, coming home
he was supposed to be
gently breathing
throughout the night
by my side
he was supposed to be here
with me
forever
but he's not
and so
the tears are there
forever

Pain

The pain comes on suddenly
while I drive
or eat dinner
or talk to a friend
the pain is terrible
it starts somewhere
in the center of my body
and radiates out
everywhere
it's the pain of being aware
of how I miss him
in that moment
the overpowering awareness
of his forever absence
and there is no one to turn to
no where to go
no getting away
no possible refuge
no stopping the pain
it sits there
enveloping me
and I am helpless in its grip
contemplating with awe
the immensity
of how much pain one can bear
without dying from it

Alone at a Party

Going alone to a party
will the people there be friendly?
will someone talk to me?
or will I stand in a corner
glass in hand
scanning the room
for a familiar face
not finding one
looking for a smile or nod
approaching close-knit groups
unable to enter?
I am a stranger among the natives
an alien in a foreign land
I will go home early tonight

Widowhood 101

I am supposed to morph
into a single person
overnight
last time I was single
I was twenty
now all of a sudden
I am single again
couplehood is the natural state of affairs
we live in a paired world
so we did everything together—
worked, played, taught, wrote, traveled
exercised, danced, walked, ate, slept
laughed, cried, were silent together
we went to movies, theaters, and concerts
we liked the same foods
and needed naps at the same time
he told me what to read in the business section
I told him what to read in the health section
we were inseparable—joined at the hip
I am trying to morph into this strange,
as-yet unknown single person
whom I don't like
who is she, this other woman
looking lost, with a new, slower step
and puffy eyes?
I don't recognize her
I don't want to know her

When Will Time Heal?

They say, "Time heals all wounds."
so I'm waiting
it's been four months
I still cry too easily
a hug, a "How are you doing?"
and I cry
they say, "It will get better."
—when?
I still just go through the motions
it still does not feel real
that he's not here
but I am still here
that I am alone
that I'm lonely
that I miss him nonstop
people are kind
but people don't understand
they say they're glad
I'm doing better
but I'm not doing better
perhaps I'll never be better
perhaps this is it
unremitting pain for the rest of my life
yet for a moment I can enjoy
a concert, a movie, a dinner conversation
but underneath it all
pervasive, but hidden from view
there is no pure pleasure
no real joy
only lurking pain
gray shadows
covering life
everything muted
with no clear sounds
and so I'm waiting
for time to start healing

Only Silence

The sweetest sound in the world
was the sound of his peaceful breathing
as he lay next to me in bed
that sound secured the night
now that there is only silence
I do not feel safe anymore

Eating Alone

The fridge is empty
I go to the market alone
carrying the groceries home
the bags are heavy
he used to carry them
it's time to eat
I don't bother
with a placemat
nor with a linen napkin
I take a sheet of paper towel
I tear off a piece of
the rotisserie chicken
cut up a tomato

a slice of bread
I don't cook anymore
it's no use, for just one
sometimes it's only
a peanut butter sandwich
or some cottage cheese with fruit
sometimes I don't even bother
to sit at the table
but stand
at the kitchen counter,
eating without pleasure,
because I'm eating alone

Good Memories

People say
"You're lucky
to have good memories"
they say
"It helps to remember"
well, it doesn't
it doesn't help at all
it just makes me
miss him more
it makes the loss
more poignant
the more wonderful the memories
the worse the aching
for what is no longer
and can never be again
I wonder what it's like
to have bad memories
I'm guessing
it's not much better

Neighborhood Shops

I went to the cleaners
for the first time since he died
my husband's obituary was on the wall
behind the cash register
so I cried
then I went to the wine shop
and said my husband has died
and so now I must buy the wine
I had never taken notice
of what my husband bought
but the salesman knew
and took out
four bottles of red
and four bottles of white
they were on sale
he will send it over
I looked at the bottles
and I cried again
in the bookstore
I was asked
how my husband was feeling
he did not look well
the last time he was there
and so I cried once more
in the familiar neighborhood stores
we had shopped at
over many years

Firsts

I can't believe
all the mundane things
he took care of
that were not
in my job description
how many "firsts"
have there been?
the first time
I figured out
how to fix the TV
program the video recorder
play DVDs
the first time
I put gas in the car
lugged heavy groceries
opened a bottle of wine
took out the garbage
pried open a stuck drawer
filled out the tax forms
renewed the newspaper
reset all the clocks
to daylight-saving time
changed a light bulb
and now a new "first" —
being sick at night alone
throwing up with no one
to bring a washcloth
give me a glass of water
and feel sorry for me
how many more "firsts"
will there be?
I'm not looking forward to them

Stuff in a Drawer

His slippers are still
by his side of the bed
his cell phone, now canceled,
is in his drawer, along with
his wallet, emptied of cards
a flashlight
a bookmark
a pad of paper
two pens, some stamps
lip balm
reading glasses
three pocket combs
a key to some unknown lock
a book
a box of unmarked pills
that I'll throw out
a rubber band
bits of string
two small buttons
to replace fallen ones
from some forgotten shirt
a senior discount movie card
(will they switch it to my name?)
some old bills
a drug prescription
left unfilled
a charger for his cell phone
that does not work
an address
a phone number
on a crumpled piece of paper
a business card

from an unknown doctor
all things left
jumbled in a drawer
of the nightstand
by our bed
things used
or about to be used
objects from an ongoing life
interrupted midstream
by death
things left up in the air
with nowhere to go
and so I stand here
sorting the stuff of daily life
wishing that the man
who was supposed to use it
were still here
wearing the glasses
reading the book
stopping to read out loud
a passage he found
particularly poetic
and so I stand here
missing the man
while sorting his stuff
aching for the man
to whom this all belonged
mementos
to be discarded
to be treasured
just stuff

Not Crying

She hugged me
and I didn't cry
he asked, "How are you?"
and I didn't cry
I came home
to my empty space,
and I didn't cry
they called to say
"We love you."
and I cried

The Birthday

The phone rings
"May we speak to Dr. Gadon?"
the cheerful voice asks
"He's not here," I reply.
"Why are you asking?"
"His credit card won't go through."
"Who is this?" I ask, puzzled.
"It's the flower shop
he had ordered flowers
three months ago
for his wife's birthday,
which is today.
Are you Mrs. Gadon?"
"I am—
my husband died almost three months ago."
"Oh, we are so sorry."
yes, me too
"You can take his name off your list."
and so I cried for the rest of the day

The Musical

A searing pain
out of the blue
I'm sitting in a theater
watching a musical
the pain is not physical
it's a terrible longing
he would have loved the play
and he's dead
so I hurt
because the play is good
if it were bad
I wouldn't be so upset
that he's not here
I should only go to events
he would not have liked
I should go to boring stuff
so as not to miss him so much
the musical was wonderful
I hated it

One Hour at a Time

There is a constant presence
of his absence
he is everywhere
yet nowhere
I do not look for him
and yet I search
I feel the emptiness
of past plenty
and still have the fullness
of what has been
I am blessed
for having had
all the world can offer
and I now feel impoverished
for having lost it all
life has lost its meaning
gone the fun of fun
the pleasure of pleasure
one day at a time?
sometimes it is just
one hour at a time
trudging through deep snow—
or is it mud, or molasses?
it is the constant presence
of his absence

Joined at the Hip

She called
her sister had died
and she was so grief-stricken
that I could leave
my own nightmare for a while
and connect to hers
we talked of love and loss
of being joined at the hip
she with her sister
and I with my husband
so that after these deaths
our limbs felt like they had been
surgically separated
bleeding and painful
the scars will make us both
limp forever

Dancing Alone

Can pleasure be pleasurable
if not shared with another?
can beauty be felt
if not pointed out?
is music more melodious
when enjoyed with someone else?
does a companion
make food taste better?
can something be funny
if not laughed at together?
can an insight be true
if it remains unconfirmed?
can a story be told
if there is no one to hear?
does one talk to oneself
in an empty room?
do we start whispering
then stop altogether?
can one dance alone
while listening to music?
everything and everyone
in the world comes in pairs
it's a coupled world
so what am I doing uncoupled
alone and lonely
not belonging to a mate
not being part of someone
floating aimlessly
in a sea of singlehood?
do we become dead
before we actually die?

People Say

People say, "He's still with you."
"No, he is not," I reply.
"He's dead."
yet last night
as I was watching
a stupid movie on TV
I imagined him reading
telling me to lower the sound
and then asking me later,
"How did it end?"
I guess in a small way
maybe, perhaps once in a while
here and there
in a very small way,
he could still be with me

A Dam Broke

It's been over six months
suddenly, searing pain
a flood of tears
not connected to anything
sitting in my room alone
I'm sobbing
what is it about?
there was no triggering event
no evocative thought
somewhere inside
a dam whose waters
had been held in check
for too long
broke
nothing in particular
made it overflow
I guess
once in a while
unexpectedly
there might be
a breach in the dam

No One to Cry With

There is no vacation
from bad news
whether personal or not
I have no one
to share it with
a good friend has cancer
another one has died
I go alone to the funeral
no one to cry with
I feel badly for victims of floods
or earthquakes or droughts
and I am alone
with my feelings
that are now bottled up
painful feelings shared
are reduced in quantity
reduced in strength
reduced

Evenings Are the Worst

Daytime is not too bad
I'm busy, mostly
with meetings, phone calls
endless paperwork
meals with friends
somehow during the day
I can keep busy
involved with people and projects
eating and chatting
but after dinner
coming back to the apartment
empty and silent
is the worst
when I close the shutters
lower the blinds
uncover the bed
I put a large teddy bear
on his side of the bed
it felt stupid at the time
but it's still there
evenings are the worst

Talking to No One

So this is it
it will never change
forever lonely
missing him
throughout the day
at odd times
I have begun
to talk to him
out loud
a few words
once in a while, like
"Where are you?"
or "I miss you, I love you"
and also "What should I do?"
and "What shall I wear?"
it is weird
talking to no one
I feel a bit nuts
but in some odd way
it is also comforting
so I won't tell anyone

Eight Months

It's been almost eight months
since he died
and I'm not doing any better
so I'm upset
about still being so upset
about tears starting to flow
unexpectedly
with no obvious trigger
during meals with friends
or working at my desk
some days I don't cry at all
other days, I cry all the time
so I went to see a therapist
to ask whether I'm depressed
she said it was normal grieving
she said I should stop fighting
fighting to get above it
for it cannot be done
should not be done
she said I should allow it
allow the tears
that get rid of the toxins
that build up
from grief unexpressed
which I still
really don't want
to express

It's Showtime!

When I am about to be with people
I say to myself
"It's showtime."
and I walk into a room
smiling, shaking hands
I say, "I'm doing fine"
lies — all lies
I'm not fine at all
I'm grieving
I'm suffering
I'm lonely
but it's showtime
and so I put on my happy face
put energy into my walk
when I really feel like slumping
like crawling, like not moving at all
instead I stand erect
look people in the eye
and proclaim
"I'm fine"
this makes everyone else happy
I have played my part
I have met expectations
it would be too embarrassing
to say, "I'm hurting"
"Lend me a shoulder to cry on"
"Let me tell you
how terrible I feel
how awful it all is"
so I say, "I'm fine"
because
it's showtime

The Mirror

My mirror is gone
I lost my reflection
the reflection that said
"You look pretty tonight"
or "You did a good job"
I could ask my reflection
"What do you think of this?"
and my reflection would respond
always with great wisdom
my reflection is gone
I no longer have that mirror
so I stare at emptiness
devoid of answers

Ten Months

Today is a bad day
it is an anniversary
a strange kind of
anniversary
it is ten months today
since he died
so I'm crying a lot
missing him
remembering
but mostly
crying a lot

Broken Toe

I was sitting barefoot
reading the paper
the phone rang
I was sure it was my husband calling
so I ran to the phone
stubbed my toe
heard the crack
it wasn't my husband
my husband is dead
but my toe is broken
went to the doctor
who took an X-ray
I said I knew
it would take six weeks
for a bone to mend
the doctor said
six weeks is for nineteen-year-olds
I said, "Oops"
so now I can't wear shoes
just flip-flops
winter is coming
I'm glad it doesn't snow
in California

Lost Memories

When parents die
one's whole childhood disappears
no one else would have witnessed
the minutiae of the growing years
there is no one
with whom to share
these early memories
when a spouse dies
one's whole adult life disappears
no one else
would have participated
in the minutiae of daily life
the trips, the work, the play
the children's and
grandchildren's stories
the friends in common
these are not remembered
together anymore
so there are huge gaps
craters of irreplaceable memories
engulfing chunks of life
never to be shared again
nor talked about
nor remembered
we lose the past
the continuity
so we keep going alone
impoverished forever

The Sunset

Early August—
the sun is setting at seven o'clock
one of the better sunsets
to the right—magenta and charcoal clouds
to the left—pink and lavender
but straight in front
streaks of the brightest orange
and so I sit on my balcony
wondering if seeing such a colorful
    extravaganza
is good for my immune system
like music is good for the brain
usually I would say, "Come see the sunset"
and we would sit, holding hands
not for too long
his back would hurt in the straight chair
and now I sit alone
missing the sharing
trying to make myself appreciate this sunset
instead I feel sorry for myself for being alone
sorry for him—for not seeing it
sorry about life's endings
as the sky darkens
the palm tree in front of our balcony
is beginning to rustle in the night breeze
it's not *our* balcony anymore
there is no *us*—no *we*
my balcony feels forlorn
the ghost of a happy couple
oblivious to the ephemeral
makes it difficult to stay
anyway, it's time to return
to the well-lit living room
and go on

Gifts of Love

If the love was great
is the loss greater?
if one has loved so well
and in turn
was so well loved
is the missing of this love
more painful than
if we had not loved as well?
or is the memory
of what I had
knowing the gift
of these years together
so powerful
and so compelling
that I can, in fact
be grateful
for what had been given
more than I mourn
what has been taken away?

The Bottle Opener

I am in my mid-eighties
and I have never, ever
opened a bottle of wine
I never had to
when I had women friends over
it was for tea and coffee
when we had couples over
my husband opened the wine
and got the ice cubes
I passed the hors d'oeuvres,
the plates, and the napkins
he got the glasses
and the bottle opener
my goal in life
is never to have to open
a bottle of wine
I will buy only Australian wines
because they come
with a twist top
so no cork to break
no gadgets to mess with
and no looking incompetent
I had a few friends over tonight
I asked one of the men
to open the wine
my husband had bought before he died
it is, after all, a man's job

The Things People Say That Don't Help

People try to help
they say
he had a long life
he had a good life

People try to help
they say
he did not suffer long
one must be grateful

People try to help
they say
you have good memories
to sustain you

People try to help
they say
he is in a better place now
he is at peace

What people say
does not help
for there is nothing
people can say
that would help
except maybe just
I'm sorry

The Scab

The wound seems to be healing
a scab covers it
my mother used to say
"Don't pick at it
or it will start bleeding again"
death is like a wound
grief, the scab
one should not pick at it
when all seems well
someone comes along
and says the wrong thing
like, "How are you coping?
He was a wonderful man.
We miss him too."
and the scab opens up,
spilling tears instead of blood
so don't pick at the scab
its crust is still too thin
and words can scratch
like a fingernail
and open it again

The Blank Page

In the grief workshop
I attended
we were asked
to divide a piece of paper in three
and find some pictures
from a magazine
to paste onto it
the first part was who we were
the second, who we are
and the third, who we will be
I picked a couple dancing
for the first
a sad, lonely woman
for the second
and left the last part blank
I do not know who I can be
who I will be
who I'm supposed to be
I can't imagine a future—
neither alone
nor with anyone else—
so that page
will remain blank

The Dopamine * Fix

I am missing my dopamine fix
I was addicted to that hormone
like to a feel-good drug
my husband gave the daily shots
in the form of compliments
in the look of admiring eyes
in the hug and the kiss
the smile of recognition
that I am loved —
but I also miss giving dopamine shots
it felt equally good
to smooth a wrinkled brow
or a down-turned mouth
to comfort, to reassure
and always to love
in return —
my dopamine fix
was not only in getting it
it was as much
in giving it

---

* Dopamine is a chemical compound found in the brain that transmits nerve impulses. It is part of the reward system of the brain, providing feelings of enjoyment.

Romeo and Juliet

Romeo and Juliet died again
last night at the opera
it was a long death scene,
and I cried,
remembering my husband
also dying slowly
with no song
with no words anymore
just with pain
and gasping breath
Romeo and Juliet
stood up and took their bows
to loud applause
my husband left on a gurney
to eternal silence

The End of Sharing

I tell a friend,
"Nick got a Fulbright to Germany."
she says, "Who's Nick?"
"He's our grandson."
I tell a friend,
"Eliot is a reporter
for the *Wall Street Journal;*
Scott got a scholarship
to Carlton College;
Ari has a great job in Boston;
Daniel got into medical school;
Laura has her own horse farm;
Nicholas is getting married."
and she says "Who?"
and I say, "Our grandchildren."
"Oh, that is great," she says, unconvincingly
but she's not really thrilled
as I wished she would be
as I know he would be
who to tell?
who's interested
in the dreams
in the hopes
in the fears?
no one to share with
one's day
one's thoughts
one's life
no one

Our Anniversary

Today is our anniversary
but no flowers
no cards
with loving words
today is the first
of many anniversaries
alone
I was warned
about the holidays
and the special days
I was warned
it would be hard
I did not know
how tough it would be
to live through this day
tears that have been absent
are lining my lower lids
waiting to spill
at the slightest opportunity
they don't need
much provocation
someone's hug
even just a "hello"
so, sitting home alone
I am missing him
even more today
our anniversary

Slow Clock

Sometimes when I wake up
I look forward to the day
usually because something
pleasant or interesting
has been planned
other times I wake up
and dread the day
a day alone
with nothing to look forward to
just sadness and heaviness
a day to get through
as best I can
trudging through the hours
with a clock whose hands
have slowed down
so what I have to do
is push myself to plan
something, anything
that will make it easier
to get through the day
something that
will help me forget—
for a while anyway—
that he is gone

What's Missing

We had plans
for aging together
holding hands
throughout the coming years
we have not only lost a past
we have lost the present
as well as a future —
the one about
two little old people
supporting each other
an arm, a cane, a walker,
maybe even a wheelchair
what's missing most
is the arm

Resignation

So this is what
it's going to be like—
a life lived alone
even though
surrounded by friends
all well-meaning
and supportive
my husband and I
had merged into each other
pathologically symbiotic
how to replace
being constantly needed
constantly needing
to share all thoughts
process all feelings
now left alone—adrift
surviving each day
looking for an anchor
looking for someone
to fill the void
a feminist once said
"A woman needs a man
like a fish
needs a bicycle"
and then she got married
do I need a man?
a voice in the silence
of my apartment
asking what I read
where I walked
who I talked to
whether I ate
how I slept
an inquiring voice
caring about the minutiae
of my daily life?
it takes a long time
to find an old friend
so this is how
it's going to be
resigning myself
to living alone
resignation
is a sad word

Tired!

Ever since he died
I have felt tired
I wake up tired
I may have a bit of energy
during the day
but then I'm exhausted
afterward
I have become a person
who drags her feet
pushes herself out of an armchair
with a sigh
I walk slower,
think slower,
and everything matters less—
the way I look,
what clothes I wear,
whether I need a haircut,
I am also more forgetful
I have to keep checking
my calendar
lest I forget to go somewhere
or do something I've promised to do
I forget who just asked me a question
or what that question was
I walk into a room
and wonder why I'm there
I mix up names and faces
and worry whether
I'm losing my mind
I wonder whether I have MCI
"mild cognitive impairment"
but maybe it's not even
"mild" anymore
yes, I'm more tired and forgetful
than I was a year ago

I Envy Couples

I envy couples
who hold hands
and those who finish
each other's sentences
who eat from each other's plates
who look at each other
across a room
reassuring the other
with fleeting eye contact
who straighten a collar
brush off a piece of lint
who are welcome
in each other's space
I envy couples
just because
they have each other
they have someone
to talk to every morning
as they wake up
and every evening
as they go to bed
I envy couples
who care
and who are always there
for each other
I envy them because
I have no one anymore

December 29

In three days
it will be a new year
and instead of saying
I just lost my husband
this year
I'll say
my husband died
last year
and it will sound
like long ago
when in fact
it feels like it just happened
yesterday

No One

I went to the opening
of a museum
remembering that a year ago
I was there with him
I saw a play
that he would have loved
I wanted to talk about it
I went out for dinner
and wished I could give him
a little of that delicious dessert
a man asked me to dance at a party
the wrong man
I read an article in the paper
I wanted to discuss
I got a letter
I got a phone call
an e-mail came
a photo of a grandchild
a joke
no one to show
no one to tell
no one to care
no one

It's Good for Me

Everything is an effort
I make myself
go out with friends
go to cultural events
because I know
it's good for me
but I must make myself do it
it's a conscious effort
I used to look forward
to all kinds of things
I don't look forward
to anything anymore
I just do it
because it's good for me

Getting More Befuddled Every Day

Boarded the bus
to go to the concert
looked in my purse
no ticket
(must still be on my dressing table)
left jacket and purse
on my seat on the bus
ran to my room
couldn't get in
(the key was in my purse
on the seat
on the bus)
ran back
just in time
the bus was leaving
the kind people
at the box office
gave me another ticket
got home
the ticket was
in my purse
getting more befuddled
every day

Not Letting Go

Having experienced such a great loss
— the loss of my husband —
losing anything else
by getting rid of
a no-longer-used object
or no-longer-worn clothes
is too painful
I have already given away
all his clothes
keeping just an old sweater
gone are
his books, his tools,
and his stamp collection
along with the mundane paraphernalia
of his life
so holding on
to what is familiar
becomes imperative
and removing anything else
from closets or drawers
becomes an insuperable task
and so it is no wonder
that I cannot give away
any of my own clothes

Widows

Lone women walking down the street
lost in thought
women eating by themselves
having cooked for one
women sleeping solitary
in a double bed
women sitting in a theater
companionless
so many women living alone
without a partner
women filling up their days
with activities
with people
trying to replace the void
left by love now gone

Caring about Not Caring

The things I used to care about
I no longer do
but I really do care
that I don't care
about the things
I used to care about

The Middle Shelf

In between high tide
and low tide
not sure which way
the tide is turning
not yet good at recognizing
the waxing or waning moon
I have lost my frame of reference
I must learn a new language
I have lost joy and hope
so I must find
a replacement
not knowing
where to look for it
still hidden from view
it must be lurking somewhere
deep underneath something
where it is dark
or high above something
where it's hard to reach
perhaps it's on the middle shelf
right in front of me
like in a grocery store
staring at me
the annoyed clerk
pointing it out
perhaps that's what I need
some clerk to show me
what I don't see
what I can't see
yet

Moods

I have never been moody
but since he died
I find myself fluctuating
from lows of desperation
not wanting to face
another day without him
to actually having a good time
laughing with friends
enjoying a good movie
and looking forward to
a fun or interesting day
the moods are unpredictable
I am buffeted
between the highs and lows
with too little respite
for simple quiet and peace
I wish for some gray areas
with no feelings at all
and perhaps no thoughts

Stuck

A few steps forward
one or two back
but it's still progress
it's easier at six months
than it was at two
and better at ten
than at six
and now it is almost a year
I don't know yet how
but I have come to believe
that time will help
it has so far
transitioning
to easier days
to better feelings
I'll just have to
stick around
to see it happen
perhaps even
to make it happen

Scars

When a scab finally heals
enough to fall off
a scar will remain
scars do not bleed
scars are what's left
of past hurts
scabs stay hidden under clothes
they are unsightly
but scars are badges of honor
of battles fought and won
of grief conquered
of life lived
I'm waiting for my scab
to fall off

Inside Me

I don't need to remind myself
that he is gone
because in a way
he isn't
he is inside me
I have incorporated him
I am poorer for the lack
of his physical presence
but I have become richer
by his continuing to exist
in me

An Incomplete Hug

I had breakfast in town
with a good friend
he drove me home
and when he got out of the car
he gave me a hug
it was a short, perfunctory hug
I needed to be held
for another few seconds
it's been so long
since I've been hugged
so I needed
something warm
and reassuring
but it was just a quick hug
like a peck on the cheek
or a wave of the hand
perhaps I should change
my expectations
perhaps I will never
be really hugged again

Parallel Universes

I live side by side
in two parallel universes
both speak a truth
in one, I am fine
going out with friends
busy with projects
enjoying a meal, a movie
able to work
able to laugh
but in the other
I am not fine
I miss him nonstop
feeling lost
without a compass
not a whole person
but half a couple
both universes
are inhabited
at different moments
yet coexist
at the same time
I do not yet know
what living in a blended universe
might be like

The Ratio

Ratios change
good days, bad days
at the beginning
right after he died
there were only terrible days
then here and there
a few hours became bearable
then a few days
the ratio started changing
as weeks went by
then months
there were more good days
until there were
fewer bad days

Yet the good days
changed color
from their former hues
of sunshine yellows
bright reds and greens
at the beginning
right after he died
the bad days
were black
then they changed to gray
and now they are
in muted colors
the good days
are paler, softer
even though
they are the good days

I Smiled Today

I smiled today
I also laughed
I had a good time
at the art fair
ate an ice cream cone
last night
for the first time
I slept well
I enjoyed my meal
is it too soon
to feel good
for a little while?
I feel guilty
about the moments
of pleasure
about moments
when I'm not in pain
can I allow myself
to feel happy?
I know he would have
wanted it for me
but still
I feel guilty

Quiet Evening

Actually, on the good days
it's not that bad
I enjoyed dinner with friends tonight
and did not think of myself
as a fifth wheel
I am sitting alone at home
and it's OK
I read, check my e-mail
watch the news on television
and don't feel lonely
the trick is to have had
a very busy day
so that I'm really tired
and don't mind
not having anyone
to talk to
little by little
I learn the strategies
of survival

Meaning Is Overrated

I told my friend
that my life
has lost its meaning
she said
"Meaning is very overrated
goals, purposes, projects
and life's missions
are more relevant
to the young;
one spoils living in the moment
by worrying about meaning"
and so I gave myself permission
to pay attention
to the moment
and enjoy it
without having to worry
about its purpose
nor its meaning

I Hummed Today

I hummed today
as I was washing dishes
an indiscriminate tune
I hummed today
as I was getting dressed
not thinking about
anything in particular
I hummed today
for the first time
in months
I must be beginning
to heal
a little bit

The Widow Thing

It has begun—
the widow thing
a married woman called
and asked what days I have open
I mentioned every evening
this coming week and the next and the next
she said, "Oh, no, I meant lunch,
just the two of us"
widows are not invited for dinner
by couples
another wife called
her husband is ill
the two of us could have dinner
widows are good for dinner
only to wives of sick or traveling husbands
thank goodness for single women friends
good for breakfast, lunch, and dinner
for in-between meals
and late-night snacks
women friends
always there for each other
women friends
are the best

Three for Dinner

When we used to get together
with another couple
we would say
let's meet at the restaurant
and we would split the bill
now that I'm alone
my friends pick me up
insist on paying for my dinner
and then take me home
I have become a burden
when we're three
two women and one man
the women tend to talk together
and he stays on the sidelines
unable to join the conversation
single women have to learn
to include men in conversation
single women must make an effort
to be entertaining
single women
live in a couples' world
where singlehood is anathema
and we can only survive
by making friends
with other single women
by having women friends
by having sisters
who will help us survive

Leaning Posts

At first
after my husband died
I felt I was always
leaning to one side
not able to stand up straight
I felt crooked, unstable
now I realize
I must have been
leaning against someone
there was support
if there had not been
people to lean against
I would have toppled over
but there were
living leaning posts
holding me up—
my family
and my friends

Possibilities

No more
wishing for the good old days
or lamenting the bad ones
instead of memories
I shall look for tasks to be accomplished
not focus on the past and its pain
nor even linger in pleasant rememberings
but instead, I will look for the possibilities
that the future may hold
live in the present
plan for the future
and not look back
embark on new adventures
for my ship has left its shores
and is disappearing over the horizon
but it can be seen arriving
on the other side
I will be there to greet it

Taking Care of Her

I must take care
of this old woman
the one with the bifocals
and the hearing aid
I must see to it
that she takes her vitamins
and the medicine for her heart
I should take her
for a walk everyday
and get her to exercise
help her make healthy food choices
and get to bed on time
I want her to eat with friends
go to movies, plays, and concerts
I must take care
of this old woman
no one else will
for she is me

A Peaceful Place

I live in a quiet place
it's a retirement community
so people are quiet
no raucous parties here
no crying babies
no shouting children
there are no roller blades
nor bouncing balls
when I open the windows
I hear the sound of the waves
on windy days
the palm fronds rustle
old friends call less often
I am beginning
to be forgotten
it is a quiet place
that I now call home

Healing Time

They say
time heals
I suppose it does
because no one could sustain
that kind of searing pain
and continue living
I have become aware
that I am hurting less
that there are good days now
I used to be grateful
for a few hours of relief
I could not fathom
that there would be a time
I could enjoy a dinner out
a movie with a friend
this time has come
I am beginning to heal
I am beginning to hope
that I can become whole again
not just half a couple
not just a widow
but an OK single person
a whole woman
maybe even
embracing life again
maybe

Yahrzeit

Today is one year
since he died
an anniversary
I lit a candle last night
said Kaddish
a prayer for the dead
that does not mention death
and today I think about my life
my life that has become
meaningless
without him
yes, I am better
I don't cry much anymore
I go to movies with friends
yet it all feels like a sham
an exercise in getting through the
    day
this is not a complaint
I know what to be grateful for:
good health
good friends

a comfortable place
where I can live
where I can write
I am not depressed
I am still grieving
a year later
I do not know
when the sad, muted colors
that still surround my world
will ever become bright again
if ever
I do not know
if I will ever look forward
to anything again
instead of just this
"one step at a time" thing
just getting through the day
which I'm still doing
especially today
I have been told
the next anniversary is easier

The Headstone

Someone called
from the cemetery
"What should be written
on your husband's headstone?"
the first words that came to mind:
wise, kind, gentle, compassionate
he was an innovative educator
a writer
a leader
adored by his wife
treasured by his children
grandchildren
brothers
sister
I have another hundred words
no, a thousand
but the black granite stone
imposes brevity
and so, just four words
to describe a man
wise, kind, gentle, compassionate

Burial

In the Jewish tradition
one must be buried
in a plain wooden casket
biodegradable
so that flesh
will mingle with earth
blades of grass
will rise to the surface
and the flowers that bloom
will continue
the cycle of life

The Grave Marker

A white cloth
over a grave marker
held down by round stones
"Who wants to uncover?"
asked the Rabbi
"Let's do it together,"
I suggested
and so we did
the brothers
the children
revealing
black granite
with his name in white
birth and death dates
whom he was loved by
just a few words to describe
a man's whole life
as we stood quietly
the Rabbi said
the prayer for the dead
each of us shared a memory
going home
to search for closure
perhaps never finding it

At the Temple

We sing, we pray
the Rabbi reads from the book
the congregation responds
we know it's our turn
when it's in italics
the about-to-be-wed couple
is congratulated
as is the about-to-be
bar mitzvah boy
we pray for the healing of the sick
the names of the recently deceased
are read
first the ones who died this week
then the ones who died
a month ago
then the ones who died
a year ago this week
my husband's name is called
I stand up with the others
the mourner's prayer
is said in unison
the Rabbi blesses us
we wish each other
a good Sabbath
Shabbat Shalom
as we move toward
the buffet table
with its coffee and cookies
and homemade cakes
I stand alone
amid the happy chatter

Scattered

My grandfather's grave
is in Berlin
having fled Russia and the communists

his oldest son
my mother's brother
not able to escape
with the rest of the family
is buried in Moscow

my other grandfather and grandmother
shot by German soldiers
are in an unmarked grave
somewhere in Lithuania

my mother's mother is buried in New York
my mother's sister rests in a grave in Paris
my parents are buried in Los Angeles
my husband lies underground in San Diego
there is a place there
for me next to him

and so we're all scattered
remnants of families
remnants of wars
gone are the people
and soon will be gone
the memories, too
there will be
no one to remember them
not even where they are buried
and then there will be no one
to remember me

Looking at Men

I caught myself
looking at men
I have not done that
in seventy years
then it used to be boys
now it's older men
in my age group
I look and wonder
whether they're married
I would like to go out
with a male companion
for a quiet dinner
perhaps a movie
that we can talk about later
I have women friends
why isn't it the same?
I'm somehow not sure
I am allowed
to feel this way
he died just over two years ago
is it too soon
for me to wish for couplehood?
am I being disloyal
to him and his memory?
I feel guilty
for catching myself
looking at men

Perfect for Me

My husband was handsome
slim, athletic
with a full head of hair
a kind smile
he was shy
and did not speak much
I had to draw him out
but when he talked
he was brilliant
he was the wisest man
I had ever met
thoughtful, caring, generous
he was perfect for me
as I was for him
I feel grateful
for all those years
I was married
to such a man

Doors

Doors have always been
closing behind me
those of youth
of successful careers
of missed opportunities
of deeds done
that could not be undone
of words said
that could not be taken back

a heavy door
just slammed behind me
that of a wonderful marriage
of love reciprocated
a door that death closed

I have knocked on these doors
banged on them
but to no avail
they can never be opened again
but I just noticed
new doors
ahead of me
open doors
I can walk through
they promise
new friendships
new words to say and write
they promise books to read
and sights to see

so I shall stop kicking
at the old, locked doors
and tiptoe
ever so gingerly
through the open ones
through these newly
opened doors

Something Has Changed

I used to dread
coming home in the evening
to silent, empty rooms
feeling so terribly alone
tonight for the first time
I looked forward to
some quiet time
in my quiet home
after a busy day
sitting down to read my mail
checking my computer
sitting down with a book
sitting alone
without feeling lonely
something has changed

Amazing

Today I have decided
that I am not half a couple
mourning the one that's gone
for I have integrated him within me
and so I am a whole person
standing on my own two feet
independent and strong
there is nothing I cannot do
for there is nothing I can't imagine
I have no fears
not of living nor of dying
I am doing the first
the best I know how
until the second stops me
hopefully in my tracks
I feel the wisdom of my years
a learning that I can use well
to make it easier for others' journeys
as mine draws to an end
I savor the moments
in ways new to me
a quietness has taken hold
like a new distance, a perspective
an understanding
I know not exactly of what
a comfort in my place
a knowing of my time
the word may be "serenity"
it exists
even in new adventures
in willingness for risks
in shoulder shrugs at failures
in smiles at foibles
and secret laughter
at the amazingness of it all

Moving On

If I can turn my house
into a home
and fix last night's leftovers
into a feast
if I can make a stranger
into a friend
then I can change loneliness
into peace and quiet
and grief
into compassion
I can move on
from feeling sorry for myself
to being there
for those in need
I cannot change
the world outside
but I can change
my world within

Surviving in a New Year

I have decided
to stop complaining
stop feeling sorry for myself
yes, I lost my husband
my best friend
my love
but
I started thinking
about my parents
my grandparents
aunts, uncles, cousins
about our coming to America
Ellis Island
not speaking English
scared
having lost everything
we survived
and I thought about
my grandmother
fleeing Russia
with three young children
to Berlin
when her husband fell ill
and died
leaving her with no money
and no friends
she learned to make hats
with her two daughters
they survived
my husband's mother
came by boat

at age fourteen, alone
in charge of her twelve-year-old
    sister
they survived
all stories of immigrant families
stories of poverty
and untold hardship
so I have decided
to stop complaining
stop feeling sorry for myself
as I live
in a lovely retirement community
surrounded by caring friends
with no worries
about my next meal
or where I'll sleep tonight
I need to remember
where I came from
I came from people
who survived all odds
their genes are in my blood
I have their DNA
and so, I'm pulling myself together
and I face today, tomorrow
and the rest of my life
with head high
tears in check
I have turned a corner
I am not sorry for myself anymore
I am surviving loss
I celebrate having known love

A Breakthrough

A friend
saw my apartment
and said,
"Your place should be shared
with someone"
and I suddenly realized
that I don't want anyone else here
I am fine living alone
and I suddenly realized
that I am not lonely anymore
I miss him
but I do not need anyone else
to fill the void
I am finally OK
being alone
I am a complete, self-sustaining,
well-grounded person
alone
but not lonely

Is the Best Yet to Come?

Am I in transition
between a life on overload
with meetings back to back
keeping myself too busy
running from one thing to another
and a life with time for reflection
with empty spaces in my day
with time for reassessment
with time to take the time
to figure out these next steps
to reinvent myself
not as an old, widowed woman
but as an energetic, wise
and fun, single person
who has been there, done it all
and who is now starting out anew
still looking forward to that
great adventure —
life?

Healing

When one is in the middle
of pain
it is impossible to envisage
a time without it
yet that time comes
unexpectedly
surprising me
by its suddenness
from an agonizingly
slow healing
to a world of brighter colors
to a lighter step
to being whole again
there is an old saying that
when someone you love dies,
the main difference is
that he is no longer
outside of you,
he is inside
I have incorporated him
I am poorer for the lack
of his physical presence
but I have become richer
by his continuing to exist
in me

Two Dreams

Two childhood dreams:
becoming a famous poet
and falling madly in love
I became a poet
and married that love
and now that he is dead
what is left
are the poems

they will have to do

Made in the USA
Columbia, SC
12 July 2022

63340545R00061